WILL HAPPINESS FIND ME ?

D0654565

TRANSLATION: CATHERINE SCHELBERT

WHY IS EVERYTHING
SO FAR AWAY?

30

WHY DOES THE EARTH
TURN FULL CIRCLE
ONCE A DAY?

8

WHAT DOES MY DOG THINK?

8 A

WHO'S GOING TO
PAY FOR MY BEER?

145

WHAT'S THE NAME
OF THIS FOREST?

2c   2/5

WHERE IS MY BED?

IS THIS   BROWN
LUMP   EDIBLE ?

WOULD IT HELP ME
IF·I DUG A HOLE?

56

ARE ANIMALS
        PEOPLE?

142

HAS THE LAST BUS GONE?

53

63

WHEN IS THE
MONEY. COMING?

WHY DOESN'T SHE CALL?

335

WHO RUNS THE CITY?

41

WHAT HAPPENED 4.56
BILLION YEARS AGO?

HOW LONG IS
THE NILE?

HOW MUCH IS

42 × 87 ?

155

WHAT GOOD
~~WHO~~ IS THE MOON?
~~GOOD FOR?~~

B   105

IS MY BEING FILLED
WITH SERENITY ?

3

SHOULD I GET DRUNK?

ANOTHER GLASS ?

IS IT OKAY TO CLOSE YOUR
EYES AND SEE ~~LANDSCAPES~~
colorful ~~ABSTRACT PICTURES~~
WHEN YOU'RE LISTENING
TO MUSIC?   IMAGES

$\sqrt{390}$

DO I HAVE TO ENVISION
THE UNIVERSE AS
FOAM?

DO WE GO THROUGH
A WALL WHEN WE
FALL ASLEEP?

26

25

~~Should I stay in bed~~

WAS I A GOOD CHILD?

23

~~AM I TOO SOFT?~~

24

IS THERE ANY
FARMLIFE LEFT
IN THE FAMILY ?

WHO'S NIBBLING ON
MY HOUSE?
LITTLE

2 C   245

AM 1 TOO GOOD TO WORK?
                                183

~~WHERE ARE MY KEYS?~~

                                1

~~HOW LONG IS THE NILE?~~ ? 86

S THE EARTH A MOTHER ?

241

. . . .

IS MY SOUL BEDDED
ON STRAW?

ON STRAW?

259

IS MY BODY A HOTEL?

SHOULD I MAKE MYSELF

96 SOME SOUP?

~~DO I HAVE TO STAY OUTSIDE?~~

95

B

WILL HAPPINESS

FIND ME?

WAS IT A MISTAKE
NOT TO RUN AWAY FROM
HOME ?

AM I A DONKEY?

~~WOULD YOU LIKE A HAMBURGER?~~

246, 247

A

IS THERE A SECRET
TUNNEL LEADING
DIRECTLY TO THE
KITCHEN?

SHOULD I MARRY
MY MOTHER ?

342

AM I MY CAR ?

122

~~AM I TRANSPARENT?~~

IS MY BRAIN A POORLY
FURNISHED APARTMENT
?

25

WHY DO I ALWAYS FALL
OUT OF BED AT NIGHT?

11B   120

DO SOULS WANDER

1C   24

ARE PEOPLE RIGHT
TO FEEL SORRY
FOR ME?

SHOULD I LIVE
IN THE WOODS AS
A ROBBER?

374

DOES THAT DOG
BARK ALL NIGHT?

22C   15

IS EVERYTHING
HALF AS BAD?

14

~~IS EVERYTHING~~
~~A DREAM?~~

~~HAS THE LAST BUS GONE?~~

B   . 52,53

91

WOULD I MAKE

A GOOD COP?

IS HUNGER AN EMOTION

?

I   97   B

AM I MUSICALLY
HOMELESS ?

HOULD I SHOW MORE

NTEREST

   IN THE WORLD?

                    310

M I A SERF OF

THE DECIMAL SYSTEM?

                               402

WHY IS IT SO QUIET
ALL OF A SUDDEN?

23   48   /

WILL INSECTS OVERTAKE US
                              ?

~~SHOULD I GO HUNTING?~~

WHY DO WE STICK
TO THE GROUND ?

~~WHAT DO THE OTHERS KNOW~~
~~ABOUT ME ?~~

WHERE IS THE
GALAXY HEADING ?

7 C   182

WHO OWNS PARIS ?

IS THE DEVIL A
CHEERFUL PERSON

417

DOES MY CAR KNOW
ME?

IS EVERYTHING IN
MY ~~HEAD?~~ ~~MIND?~~ ?

SHOULD I SLAUGHTER
MY PIG ?

WHAT DRIVES ME?

WHEREWILL I END UP TODAY

125

18B

CAN MUSIC BE USED
TO CALM ME DOWN ?

10   39

IS EVERYTHING I HAVE
EVER FORGOTTEN AS
BIG AS A HOUSE?

223

SHOULD I MAKE MYSELF
AVAILABLE FOR
RESEARCH?

11

DO I KNOW *ALMOST* ~~EVERY-~~
THING ABOUT MYSELF?

27   A   276

AM I FRITTERING
AWAY MY LIFE?

IS MY IGNORANCE
A ROOMY CAVE?

202/203

HOW DO I COME ACROSS?

~~HOW DO I LOOK?~~

DO OPINIONS COME
ON THEIR OWN   ?
                    3

AM I LOVED ?

30 B   6

WHY DON'T THEY
LEAVE ME ALONE?
          (IN PEACE!?)

IS THE WORLD THERE
WHEN I'M NOT?

SHOULD I WALK AROUND
IN RAGS?

44

4

AM I ONE OF
THE CHOSEN?

WHY ARE THERE
BAD
PEOPLE?

COULD I HAVE BECOM
SOMETHING ELSE ?

27

IS FREEDOM ALIVE ?

42

DOES   PIGHEADED
WISHING HELP?

4 28

'S RESISTANCE USELESS ?

3 7 5
4 2 8

AM I AN ODDBALL?

22 81

ARE FASHIONS A PLAGUE

~~ARE FASHIONS AN~~
~~LIFE EMPTINESS?~~

~~HOW GOOD IS MY HIDEOUT~~

IS IT POSSIBLE TO DO
EVERYTHING WRONG?

435

A

SHOULD I LET MYSELF
GO?

294

~~WHY~~ WHY IS EVERYBODY
SO NICE ALL OF A
SUDDEN ?

~~IS EVERYTHING MEANINGLESS~~
1/2/87

WHY DOES NOTHING

NEVER HAPPEN?

320

AM I INVISIBLE TO GHOSTS?

~~CAN GHOSTS SEE ME?~~

AN GHOSTS SEE
ME ?

25

HAVE I EVER BEEN
COMPLETELY AWAKE ?

IS SLEEPING THE ONLY
WAY TO FIGHT FATIGUE

258

AM I CAUGHT

IN·A WEB?

27

IS A WITCH
RIDING ME?

89

SHOULD I SMOKE OPIUM?

25

DO WE SEE THE
DARK SIDE OF THE
WORLD ON TELEVISION
AT NIGHT?

WHY DOES IT TAKE THE EART
EXACTLY ONE YEAR
TO CIRCLE AROUND
THE SUN?

SHOULD I VISIT ALIEN
GALAXIES IN
MY SPACESHIP?
WITH

377

DO I HAVE TO IMAGINE
DEATH AS A LANDSCAPE
WITH A HOUSE THAT YOU CAN
WALK INTO AND THERE'S
A BED TO SLEEP IN?

SHOULD I BUILD A HUT
IN THE WOODS AN LIVE
THERE ALONE ~~WU~~
IN POVERTY?

30C   26°

WHOSE ~~BITTER~~ FATIGUE
DO I FEEL ?

368

IS IT MORE IMPORTANT
FOR THE WORLD OR FOR
ME TO BE DOING WELL?

WHAT'S IN A DOG
THAT ENJOYS LYING
IN THE SUN? 337

DOES PROFOUND PEACE
PREVAIL AT HOME WHEN
I'M NOT THERE ?

372

IS TWO TIMES TWO
PROBABLY FOUR?

349

SHOULD I LEAVE
REALITY IN PEACE?

367

DOES COZINESS LEAD
STRAIGHT TO
DISASTER ?
(AND CRIME ?)

~~AM I BORED ?~~

AM I TOO WELL GROOME
?

AM I TOO SOFT?

SHOULD I SHUN
THE LIGHT OF
THE DAY ?

3.

ARE COW SHEDS THE
FOUNTAIN OF
COZINESS ?

HOW SHOULD I
DECORATE MY TREE?

61

RE THE ALIENS
GOING TO ABDUCT
S TO PARADISE?

[220

IS A GHOST MARCHING
NEXT TO ME?

28

SHOULD I BUY A STRONG LAMP?

~~SHOULD I AVOID DAYLIGHT?~~

HOW THICK IS THE FOG?

208, 209

IS SHE CARRYING A
WEAPON?

206

IS MY STUPIDITY
A WARM COAT?

202

WHY DOES EVERYTHING
REVOLVE AROUND ME?

304

CAN I STILL DRIVE?

252

DO I LIKE A
GOOD BRAWL?

CAN I, MAY I
DO EVERYTHING?

WHERE DOES THIS TRAIL
OF BLOOD LEAD   ?

WHY IS THE FOREST
SILENT?

RE WE LOSING
CONTROL ?

78 B

CAN I TWIST AND TURN
EVERYTHING THE WAY
I WANT ?

WHAT DO THEY KNOW
ABOUT ME ?

S

SHOULD
I EAT CHALK ?

DID I SAY SOMETHING
WRONG YESTERDAY?

47

DO I HAVE TO STAY
OUTSIDE?

365

DO WE HAVE TO LOOK
AT THINGS SOBERLY?

26   A 7

DOES EVERYTHING
TAKE CARE OF
ITSELF ?

                                        124

20 B

WAS
AM I GROSS?

151

4 C

WHERE IS THE NEAREST
POLICE STATION?

WHAT PERCENTAGE OF ME
ANIMAL ?

17

WHY DO THEY HOUND
ME ON ALL THE
CHANNELS AT NIGHT ?

43.

SHOULD I LAUNCH

AN

INVESTIGATION?

262

ISN'T EVERYTHING

ALWAYS

GAINST ME?

136

SHOULD I
SWALLOW LESS?

WHY DO THEY KEEP
FILMING ME AROUND
THE CLOCK?

WHY DO I ALWAYS
HAVE TO FIGHT ?

98

Z B

COULD WE COMPLAIN
ABOUT MOST THINGS ?

V

133

IS SHE DRUNK ?

2◦

SHOULD I SOW MALICE
HATRED, AND SPITE ?

3◦

WHY DO I ALWAYS
KNOW BETTER?

3B   107

WHY DOESENT ANYBODY
PPRECIATE THAT I BEHAVE
NORMALLY?

                              311

AM I JUSTIFIABLY
CONCEITED, VAIN,
AND COMPLACENT

388

IS THE STENCH COMING
FROM OUTSIDE?

17

SHOULD I INVADE
RUSSIA ?

113

HOULD I PUNISH THE

ORLD BY   IGNORING

IT ?

~~WITH IGNORANCE~~ ?

348

WILL CHILDREN SING
SONGS ABOUT ME
IN A HUNDERD YEARS

303

SHOOLD I SATISFY
MYSELF?

331

OES **NT** EVERYTHING ON
ELEVISION HAVE
OMETHING TO DO
ITH ME ?

178

AM I BEAUTIFUL ?

275

AM I A BLOATED
WIND BAG ?

IS EVERYBODY ELSE GRAZ

16 C   132/139

IS MY STOMACHACHE

BAD ENOUGH TO
CALL IN SICK ?

324

ARE ~~EMOTIONS~~ MY FEELINGS
DETERMINED BY
BODILY FLUIDS?

6

CAN THE PRINCIPLE
OF YEAST BE APPLIED
TO A LOT OF OTHER
THINGS?

IS THE REALM OF
POSSIBILITY GETTING
SMALLER AND SMALLER
?

IS MY DIGESTIVE SYSTEM
A WONDERFUL THING?

286

S MY WEB OF LIES A
1ASTER PIECE OF INNOVATION
AND ENGINEERING?

IS ANY MEANS JUSTI-
FIED TO STAVE OFF
A BAD MOOD?

114

AM I BEING
EXPLOITED?

205

WHY AM I ALWAYS
RIGHT ?

106

IS IT PRESUMPTUOUS
TO ASK *FOR* A LITTLE SOUP
AFTER A HARD DAY'S
WORK ?

18

WE

DO I HAVE TO ~~HAVE~~

~~HAVE~~ DO PENANCE

FOR ~~EVERYTHING?~~

EVERYTHING

37A

CAN SOMETHING

BE UNBELIEVABLE

212

8

SHOULD I GET DRUNK ?

64

WHY DO THEY WANT TO
KNOW WHERE I WAS
YESTERDAY AT 2:30pm ?

137B

AM I DOOMED TO WANDER
THROUGH
THE VALE OF TEARS AS
A CLOWN?

14

IS IT TIME FOR
AN OVERTHROW?

57

AN TRUTH DO ?
   WHATEVER IT WANTS

   ·· GET AWAY WITH
         EVERYTHING ?

356

DO FACTS CHECK
UP ON ME?

SHOULD I PAY LESS
ATTENTION TO MY
WORRIES?   28

                                  28

WHY DOES THE WORLD AFFOR
THE LUXURY OF HAVING
ME?

DO FACTS CHECK UP ON ME?

M I BEING SNUBBED ?

COULD I BE JAPANESE ?

DO I NEED SOMETHING SWEET

?

ARE FEELINGS PRIVATE?

383

27

HY DO I LET MYSELF
E ORDERED AROUND?
ALL THE TIME?

140

SHOULD I TRASH
EVERYTHING?

141

5C

ARE THEY EATING
EVERYTHING AWAY
FROM ME ?

253

AM I A LOUSY, STINK-
ING RAT ?

221

28A

DO I HAVE TO MAKE
MYSELF CLEARER ?

219

C

WHY IS EVERYONE   ELSE
ALWAYS BETTER OFF ?

60

CAN I LET MY WIFE
ADMIRE THE CRIMINALS
SHE SEES ON
TELEVISION?

WILL THEY BLAME ME
FOR EVERYTHING?

17

AM I ABUSING MY
POWER?

SHOULD I LIE?

A   33

IS IT OKAY FOR MY
FEELINGS TO IGNORE
MY RESERVATIONS?

481

WHY CAN'T I SIT STILL?

17 C   15

TRULY
WHY CAN'T I BE REALLY
              CHEERFUL

DO I HAVE TO BE
           CHEERFUL ?

WHY DO I ALWAYS
AGREE WITH EVERYTHING ?

S EVERYTHING

A HOPELESS
SHITTY MESS ?

STILL

~~AM I GOOD FOR ANY-~~
~~THING?~~

AM I GOOD FOR
ANYTHING ?

SHOULD I GO TO
ANOTHER CITY AND
RENT AN APARTMENT
UNDER A FALSE NAME

IS IT DANGEROUS TO
DREAM OF ANOTHER
LIFE ALL THE TIME ?

M I NEEDLESSLY
ORTURING MYSELF ?

266

DO I HAVE TO GO THROUG

ALL OF THAT AGAIN?

30

DO THINGS (JUST) NOT
HAPPEN SLOWLY
ENOUGH? ~~FAST~~

3

TERRIBLY
DID SOMETHING GO WRONG
OR ME
SHORTLY AFTER THE
BIG BANG ?

103

SHOULD I BE
PUT IN CHAINS ?

~~WOULD IT BE BETTER FOR ME~~ .

m

SHOULD I PUT MYSELF
UNDER SURVEILLANCE?

3

SHOULDN'T I BE ASHAME
OF THINGS THAT HAVE
NOTHING TO DO WITH ME

4/

WILL SOMETHING
LEAK OUT ?

IS THE WORLD
FULL OF SECRET
MESSAGES ?

SHOULD I PAY LESS
ATTENTION   TO MY
WORRIES ?

291

SHALL I GO UNDER ?

43

6

AN I RE-ESTABLISH
MY INNOCENCE?

~~BEINGS IN OUTER SPACE~~ ?

AM I A ~~LIKE~~ SPONGE ?

21 C   15:

AM I TAKING THE
WRONG DRUGS ?

32(

MUST I BE ASHAMED
OF HAVING NO
OPINION ABOUT
MOST THINGS ?

308

IS THE FREEDOM
OF BIRDS OVERRATED
?

394

IS MR. INSANITY
    AT THE DOOR?

165

SHOULD I SECRETLY
RENT A ROOM IN
FAIRFIELD?

2

AM I SOMEBODY ELSE IN PRIVATE?

K4

SHOULD I PUT MY WELL-BEING AT THE CENTER OF MY ACTIVITIES?

263

WHAT IS IN MY
APARTMENT WHEN
I'M NOT THERE?

SHOULD I BUILD MYSELF
A WORLD OF ILLUSION?

DO GALAXIES
SEPARATE ME
FROM THE OTHERS ?

289

CAN EVERYTHING
BE THOUGHT?

5   A 216

COULD I PUT MY EVERLASTI

EFFORTS TO APPEAR NORMA

TO BETTER USE?

WHY IS EVERY BODY

SO NICE ALL OF

A SUDDEN?

IS THE DEVIL
PLEASED WITH ME ?

135

S THE WORLD AS IT IS
PART OF A CONSPIRACY ?

225

WHY AREN'T THE STARS
DISTRIBUTED MORE
EVENLY?

HAVE ALIENS BEEN

LIVING AMONG US

~~AS~~ IN YOGURT FOR

A LONG TIME.?

IS IT TRUE THAT TRACES OF ALIENS HAVE
BEEN FOUND IN YOGURT?   4

AM I MY SOUL'S
SLEEPING BAG?

94

WHY IS EVERYTHING
SO RADIANT?

257

DO I HAVE TO ASSUM

THAT TIME IS A WORM

321

IS THERE A MISTAKE AROUND

TODAY THAT'S AS BIG

AS THE IDEA OF THE

EARTH BEING FLAT?

KB

ARE THE EDGES
OF REALITY
DIFFUSE . ?

68

WHY DO I LIVE
IN AN ANIMAL BODY ?

IS MY BODY A HOTEL ?

173,174

SHOULD I PAINT A PIRATE
SHIP ON MY CAR WITH AN ARMED
WOMAN ON IT HOLDING A
DECAPITATED HEAD BY
THE HAIR?

420

AM I A FARMER
IN WINTER?

12 B

11

SHOULD I STAY IN BED?

238

ARE MY BODY JUICES OKAY?

~~DOES (ALMOST) EVERYTHING~~
~~HAVE TWO SIDES?~~

4

ARE THERE NO LIMITS
TO THE IMPOSSIBLE?

126

CAN REALITY STILL BE DESIG-
NATED AS SUCH?

~~WHERE IS MY BED?~~

38A   67/85

AN'T I SEE

A SIGN BEHIND

VERY CORNER?

386

IS SEVEN A LOT?

MI CONNECTED WITH
~~EVERYTHING~~?

~~IS EVERYTHING LIQUID~~?

SHOULD I ROAM, DAZED
AND DRIFTING, AROUND
THE NEIGHBORHOOD?

SHOULD I SWITCH
OVER TO THE INVIS-
IBLE WORLD?

DO I NEED ^ABSOLUTE^
PEACE AND
QUIET ?

WHAT'S WAITING FOR
US IN THE DEPTHS
OF THE UNIVERSE ? 210

IS EVERYTHING
DRIFTING
APART?

~~ARE COUNTRIES~~
~~LIVING CREATURES~~

IT IS HARD TO
IMAGINE AN EMPTY
UNIVERSE?

SHOULD I TAKE
DRUGS ON
SCIENTIFIC
GROUNDS ?

213

SHOULD I SLOWLY
SNEAK AWAY?

109

SHOULD I TAKE A WALK
OUTSIDE AT NIGHT
IN A STORM
IN WINTER WITH A
FEVER AND WEARIN
WET CLOTHES?

IS IT STILL POSSIBLE
TO LIVE IN A CAVE
NOWADAYS, WITH
NO ELECTRICITY?

WAS IT A MISTAKE TO
LEAVE MY HOME AND
STRIDE OUT INTO THE
WORLD EXPECTANTLY?

IS IT STILL POSSIBLE
TO LIVE IN A CAVE
WITH A STRANGE,
WILD WOMAN ?

3

IS MY MIRROR ENOUG
CONTACT WITH THE
OUTSIDE WORLD?

SHOULD ~~PEOPLE~~ BE
STRICTER, HARDER
AND COLDER? ~~TO ME~~?

4,3

~~HOW MUCH FOR EVERYTHING~~
~~AT MACYS~~?

WOULD IT BE ILLEGAL
TO EAT NEANDERTHALMEAT?

117/118

AM I STUFFED?

~~AM I FLYING~~?

l o C

DOES BEING TIRED
HELP TO UNDERSTAND
SECRET MESSAGES?

IS THERE ANYTHING
~~HUSEFUL~~ FOR SCIENTISTS
LEFT TO
FIND OUT ABOUT ME
?
387

SHOULD I HAVE SOMEBODY
POLISH UP MY
APPEARANCE ?

FOR A FEE ?

ARE MY FEELINGS
APPROPRIATE ?

28

AN SHE TELL ?

272

~~UNDER CONSTANT ATTACK~~

RE ILLUSIONS FRUSTRATED

Y THE COLDNESS OF

HE WORLD ?

399

IS ^(MY) INDECISIVENESS
PROOF OF ^(MY) FREE WILL

Should

CAN I BE HAPPY
WITH MY HEAD?

340

COULD ~~THEY USE ME~~ THEY USE ME
IN A GOOD MOVIE?

364

OULD I LIKE TO BE A
MYSTERIOUS PERSON,
ULL OF SECRETS?

93

HAVE THEY FINISHED
MAKING ME CONFORM

SHOULD I HAVE A
GOOD
PHOTOGRAPHER TAKE
A GOOD PICTURE
OF ME ?

WHY IS MY BLANKET
SO HEAVY
?
, 146

SHOULD I BUY
A BIG HAMMER?

254

B

AM I SUFFERING
FROM GOOD TASTE?

168

HAVE THEY KEPT MY
NOBLE ORIGINS A
SECRET FROM ME?

251

OES A DULL GLOW
ETTLE ON ME WHEN
WATCH TV?

380

433

ARE MOST THINGS
CONNECTED WITH
VERYTHING ELSE?

DO COZINESS AND
ELEGANCE GO
THEIR SEPARATE
WAYS ?

HAVE I NEVER BEEN
COMPLETELY AWAKE?

IS EVERYTHING WORSE
THAN IT USED TO BE?

434

IS SHE SULKING?

244

DO I HAVE TO GET UP
AND GO TO WORK?

323

AM I LEADING
A MODERN LIFE?

IS THE WORLD AS HARD AND
COLD AS RAW CONCRETE?
IS THE COLDNESS OF THE

WORLD BEST RENDERED

IN RAW CONCRETE?

WHAT DOES MY SOUL
DO WHEN I'M AT WORK
?

315

CAN I OPEN UP A STORE
WITHOUT KNOWING
WHAT I WANT TO SELL?

DO SPIDERS WEAVE
THEIR WEBS BY ~~EE~~
TOUCH?

SHOULD I FLY TO
INDIA IN A BALLOON?

190

A

AN'T SOMEBODY
ESLE DO THAT
FOR ME?

115

IS LIFE A STRANGE
SYSTEM OF CAVES ?

34

SHOULD I GIVE
EVERYTHING AWAY
AND ROAM THE
WORLD AS A BEGGAR ?

23

DOES MY CAR GET
FILLED WITH FEELINGS
WHEN I DRIVE?

291

HOW LITTLE CAN I
WORK AND STILL CALL
THE REST OF MY
TIME FREE TIME?

353

DOES A GHOST DRIVE
MY CAR AT NIGHT?

ARE COUNTRIES
LIVING CREATURE
?

VAS MY BATH TOO HOT?

104

RE MY FELLOW HUMAN
EINGS AT MY MERCY?

4 16

IS CARELESSNESS
GOOD FOR MELANCHOLY

IS ~~FREEDOM ALIVE~~?

76/7

234

SHOULD I BUY A GUN?

~~WAS IT ALL A COINCIDANC~~

7¢

235

SHOULD I REMOVE MY
MUFFLER AND DRIVE
ROUND THE
NEIGHBORHOOD
    AT NIGHT ?   301

SHOULD I ADD SOME
ILL WILL TO MY
PLEASANT NATURE ?

SHOULD I PUT SOME
PERFUME ON?
    AND LIGHT A CANDLE?

                        3

                    ARE   33
                THERE FALSE
                    FEELINGS?

IS THERE SUCH A THING
    AS BAD MUSIC?

                            33

ARE PEOPLE
FLOWERS?

409

IS MY SOUL THE GHOST
THAT DRIVES   MY CAR
AROUND AT NIGHT?

316

DO I HAVE TO IMAGINE
SUBATOMIC SPACE AS
SOMETHING HUGE AND DAR
AND SILEN
THAT YOU CAN CLIMB
DOWN INTO ?

22

WHY WON'T THEY
LET US TALK ABOUT
THINGS WE DON'T
UNDERSTAND?

302

DOES MY SOUL EVER
DRIVE AROUND THE
NEIGHBORHOOD AT
NIGHT WITHOUT A
MUFFLER?

316

DOES MY SOUL
LIVE IN A FAR-OFF
LAND ?

WHAT DOES MY MUFFLE
DO WHEN I DRIVE
AROUND WITHOUT IT
?

WHAT HAPPENS TO ALL ?
THE TV SHOWS I DON'T SEE

WAS THE CLOWN
EVEN REAL ?

SHOULD I WEASEL
MY WAY OUT OF
EVERY DECISION?

389

WAS THERE SOMEONE
IN MY ROOM?

DOES MY SOUL
WATCH THE TV SHOWS
MISSED IN A FOREIGN
COUNTRY ?

WOULD ANYBODY LOOK
FOR ME IF
I DISAPPEARED?

398

WHAT'S DOZING
IN SECRET ?

19

WHAT ARE THOSE GLOOM
FIGURES DOING IN THE
TWILIGHT AT THE END
OF THE STREET?

DOES UNEASE ~~STOP~~
GROW BY ITSELF?

400

HOULD I CRAWL INTO MY
ED AND STOP PRODUCING
HINGS ALL THE TIME?

404

IS THE ENGINE
WARMING UP
TO
~~FOR~~ ME ?

378

AM I A CLEAN,
WELL-OILED
MACHINE ?

218

LITTLE TRAIN
IS THERE A TO MAKE ME OUT
WAY OUT OF THIS mess
THAT ~~SHIT~~ GOES THROUGH
THE DIRT
? 401

IS THE NICE THING
ABOUT WORKING THAT
THERE'S NO TIME
LEFT? 406

DOES REALITY
REALLY DESERVE
SUCH DISTRUST?

293

IS HAPPINESS LOOKING
FOR ME IN THE WRONG
PLACE ?

© PETER FISCHLI   DAVID WEISS,
VERLAG DER BUCHHANDLUNG WALTHER
KÖNIG AND KOENIG BOOKS LTD,
LONDON.
DESIGN: P. FISCHLI D. WEISS
REPRODUCTION WORK: FARBANALYSE
COLOGNE. PRINT: OFFIZIN ANDERSEN
NEXÖ, LEIPZIG
PRINTED IN GERMANY

SPECIAL THANKS TO:
STEPHANIE DORSEY, FELICITY LUNN
JÖRG V. WALTHER, JUSTEN LADDA

DISTRIBUTION OUTSIDE EUROPE
D.A.P. / DISTRIBUTED ART PUBLISHERS IN
NEW YORK 155 SIXTH AVENUE
NEW YORK, NY 10013
TEL: 212-627-1999 FAX: 212-627-9484

ISBN 3-88375-723-3